Some Things are Better Left Unsaid

Milo Grey

AuthorHouse™
1663 Liberty Drive
Bloomington, IN 47403
www.authorhouse.com
Phone: 833-262-8899

Because of the dynamic nature of the Internet, any web addresses or links contained in this book may have changed since publication and may no longer be valid. The views expressed in this work are solely those of the author and do not necessarily reflect the views of the publisher, and the publisher hereby disclaims any responsibility for them.

Any people depicted in stock imagery provided by Getty Images are models, and such images are being used for illustrative purposes only.
Certain stock imagery © Getty Images.

This book is printed on acid-free paper.

ISBN: 978-1-6655-4816-8 (sc)
ISBN: 978-1-6655-4817-5 (e)

Print information available on the last page.

Published by AuthorHouse 12/30/2021

authorHOUSE®

Contents

Outcast

My tears are like electric pulses
Surging through my eyes
Triggered by the lies
Of the glass Window

Cheated, robbed, I feel helpless
Furthest along, and they don't even notice
Stop! Quit! Waste of time!
As if my false reality is a crime
A scope for the Window, how picturesque

Release from reality, from bounds of time and space
Out of place--Outcast
Abandoned on the shores of Time
The lonesome soul has found a home
To which escape and freedom to roam
Imagination

Close your eyes
Imagine
Not a single star is left
None shining a glimmer of hope
Through the Window
Is this the end?
Consumed by darkness
Drifting in nothingness
Outcast

Closure

What a miserable time
Waking up, 5:30 sharp chime
Verbal abuse the least of my worry
Trying to make it through the day in a hurry

At the end of my wits
Can only take so many hits
Almost ended it all
But She saved me from my fall

New place, new faces
Taking it step by step, small paces
She was drawn to me
When I needed Her most, a fated decree
She pulled me out of the black hole
I threw myself into--Oh! what a toll
Days to weeks, She became something more
I fell in love with that two timing whore

I thought She was the One
But now I'm over it, done
I gave Her love and affection
But she turned the other direction

Reconnected after a year
Got more involved, what an ordeal
Until that fated day arrive
My love for Her made a nosedive

She hung me out to dry like a useless towel
I gave Her my heart and She threw it out foul
The worst is that She doesn't even know
She saved me just to throw me right back into that hole

I hope She reads this bit about Her
Because then I might finally achieve some Closure

Water

Sprout from the ground
High above the clouds
Ice cold
Trickling down
Farther farther
Forming a stream
Listen
Soothing melody
Bliss
Flowing down
Farther farther
Rapid river
Roar of Poseidon
Water crashing
Frothy white foam
Rushing down
Farther farther
Faint rumble
Ominous roar
Waterfall
Closer
Louder
Just over the edge
Falling
Crash!
Calm
Serene
Bliss

Buoyant Faith

I feel awake in my slumber
The morning comes and
My mind drifts in
And out of REM
Like the shutters
Of a summer home
On a windy day

The comforter
Feels pleasantly soft
On my skin
Encompassing my entirety
I drift away
Before I can stir up

She is always there
With me
When I wake up
Waiting in my thoughts
To brighten my morning
But the moment
Is fleeting

She is not here
I drift away
Slumber induced
Once more
--I am alone

Mind Games

I find it remarkable,
The human mind
Capable of almost
Infinite feats
--Both evil and good

It shuts off for a third
Of our lives
Only when we sleep.
But once awake
It becomes
An organic machine

Math and language
Literature teeming
On my mind,
There is but one
Faulty quality

What of another
Mind
A rival of wits
To hear the thoughts
Of a fellow man
--What power

No man is great enough
To command such power.
Lust for dominance
Will corrupt all minds,
Beckoning the end of times

…I find it remarkable,
The human mind

Cancun Flame

I could tell you liked me
I noticed you about day three
--Walking out onto the beach
The Sun was bright
In the midday sky

I glanced over to you
Seductively reaching down
For a towel
Almost slow motion
Your cleavage aroused me
In a frost white bikini
--She had an enticing piercing
Right above her naval

You played volleyball with us one day
We were on opposite teams
I didn't mind—engorging on your
Beauty
Mustering my fortitude,
I spoke to her on New Year's Eve

Dancing with you was timeless
Your body contoured to mine
As if we were layers
Of sheets on a bed
--My hands caressed her hips
Teasing at the lining of her skirt
I started to nibble at her neck

Her room had a fleeting musk of a cat
And the perfume she had on earlier
--It was pungent and smelled of hibiscus
My lips pressed against hers without notice
Her tongue twirling mine with titillating teases
I could not contain myself

I gazed into her eyes
As I thrusted
Holding down her arms
By the wrist
Her back started arching
As I quickened the rhythm

Her moaning was joined
By my heavy breathing
I fondled her breasts
Slowly making my way
Down

I wasn't down long
Before we started again
Suckling her ample bosom
And her encouraging,
Spurring sighs
Heightened my senses
Beyond return

Watching the sun rise
With her by my side
--Our passion burned
As bright as the Sun that
New Year's Day

Organic Symbiosis

I opened my eyes,
Setting a lethargic gaze
At the sunlight
Radiating through
The canopy of trees
In the yard,
Like grains of sand
Streaming between my fingers

There was a light breeze
--Swiftly cascading
Over my skin
Invigorating my being
The cedars swayed
To and fro

Nostalgia of
The Chesapeake shores
Invade my memory
As I indulge
In a familiar
And welcoming
White noise
Of waves crashing
Onto the coast

A bird begins to chirp,
Singing a duet
--Her partner
Covertly responding
Through the awning
Of leaves.
The call and response
Calms my mind
As I breathe in
Nature

I chuckled to myself,
Half expecting to wake up
From the pleasant dream
Skeptical that life
Was truly this beautiful

I was soon subdued,
Serenaded
By Mother Nature
Cast into
A bottomless torpor

Cast Away

Words cannot express
The solemn darkness
That consumes my heart.
Opening the window
To my soul
--Rushing in
A phantom pain
It cannot be extinguished

I long for
Companionship
--The yin to my yang
But these feelings
Are only met with
Judgement and denial

It gets hard to breathe
I feel like I'm drowning
In a sea of saline.
I stand up
Only to be struck down
Once more
Again and
Again

So naïve
Too trusting
--This is who I am
Wandering
Through the desert,
Lost
I happen upon a stream,
Ladling the cool water
To my parched lips

Before the onset of relief
The water turns to sand
In my mouth.
But I continue to pour
Allowing the sand
To fill my lungs,
Making it hard
To breathe again

This time I stay down
This time I don't get up
The sand cascades over me
Forming a tomb
Where I used to greet others
They now walk over me.
Unbeknownst to them
No longer in this plane
Of existence
Lost

Desolation

The pain is always there
To remind me
That I am weak.
Sorrow builds,
Assaulting my every being
I relinquish myself,
Paralyzed by
The dissenting voice
--It echoes through
The recesses of my mind
Descending me
To unknown depths

I cannot fathom
Escalating this incessant pit
Into which I have cast myself.
The light, ever faint
It vaguely glimmers,
Projected onto the flushed walls
Of my subliminal vault.
Intangible
Seemingly growing more distant,
Efforts to escape are futile

I now welcome
The darkness,
The oblivion suits
My damaged soul.
Laying sprawled
On the cold, agonizing floor,
I beseech the fluorescence
To intensify,
To turn its gaze on me
To Incinerate my entirety

The light does not change,
It remains above
Elusive and unobtainable.
My faculties begin to dissolve,
I hear the screams
Of a broken man.
The shrieks echo,
Rebounding off the walls
Of my capacious dungeon
--They are of my own formation

I cannot comprehend
The end of my screeches
With the beginning
Of my echoing voice.
The floor beneath
Crumbles away,
Thrusting me
Into the void

The screams become distant
The light minimizes
Into a point
Before receding
Into nothingness.
I slowly drift away,
Watching my prison
Disappear,
Consumed by the darkness.

There is nothing now
Void space surrounds me,
It encompasses me
Like a lone bubble
In a glass of water.
I attempt to speak,
But my ears cannot hear.
The panic soon subsides
As I accept my fate,
Perpetually floating
To an eternal destination
Abandoned and forgotten

The Lonesome Road

An hour past the Devil's
Gazing out of the glass window,
I rest my eyes on a lone sedan.
Idle, it patiently waits
A red to green flash nigh.

An extended period of time passes
As I analyze the sky-blue finish.
The iconic three-pronged star,
It glistens underneath the red glow.
The windows are tinted pitch black.

Who hides behind such darkness?
A mysterious figure can barely be identified.
Woman or man, it cannot be discerned
Heisenberg Uncertainty crosses my mind
As it occurs to me—Why wait for no one?

A sole motorist obeys the law of the light
As if decreed by the Gods themselves.
Driving through would save time
No others around to witness the crime,
Yet here this person remains at ease.

It is relatable after some consideration,
Because I, too, refrain from rolling through.
Watching each LED, bright with crimson red
I ponder on why I am still alone
Recalling past flames—diminishing rapidly from thought.

I return from a deep meditation,
Still gazing, mouth agape from my hidden spot
The light changes green—the driver slowly accelerates
Continuing alone along their path
As I continue alone along my path.

The Way I Love

The way your wavy hair
Looks just after combing it,
Slowly cascading over your shoulders

The way your light brown fade
Compliments your pitch-black waves
In perfect harmony

The way your mesmerizing beauty
Can make any plain outfit
Look marvelous

The way we cuddle;
How the contours of your voluptuous figure
Become one with my own

The way your sexy body feels,
Slowly caressing your curves
As I fiddle with your navel ring

The way we get along so easily,
And how the only emotion I feel
With you is pure happiness

The way your cheerful personality
Blends so easily with mine;
Instantly blossoming our romance

The way your wonderful music taste
Compliments my own;
Words cannot express my excitement

The way you make me feel warm inside,
I cannot fathom life without you now;
It would deeply depress me

There is but one thing that
These facts have in common,
And that is of course
The way I love you

Airplane Mode

Speeding past illuminated markers scattered amidst the grass,
The plane departs with a frightful roar.
Ears crackling under pressure,
I turn my attention through the looking glass.

I gaze upon the houses and roadways below,
So calm and serene from my elevation.
I let my eyes wander past the canopy of trees,
Far into the distance where the sky meets the sea.

My mind begins to wonder;
How varied will this landscape appear in a decade.
Change happens so rapidly these days,
I speculate a flux of construction is certain.

We pass through the clouds now;
They float by as if transparent to this world.
Cruising altitude is upon us soon,
As I drift into a deep slumber.

Void

Perpetually falling
Through the abyss,
Boundless chasm
Dreadfully in pursuit

The tempestuous vortex;
Continuously
Pushing and pulling
Against my Being

Escape is but inches away
Yet it slips from my grasp
As if an entity controls my movements
Refusing to allow my escape

The only Salvation is present
Deep within my heart
An emblazoned silver sword
Unsheathed from my chest, hacking at my binds

Brandished with sword in hand,
I expel my tethers and rush
Towards the top
Inches from Freedom

The Light fades,
Disappearing from the
Horizon, the sword
Dissolving in hand

I awake from the nightmare,
Still tethered and unaware
Accepting the fate
Trapped in Oblivion

Airport Asphyxiation

I never really did like airports,
The exchange of people
to different places.
I hate all the hustle and bustle
Even driving to and fro,
It causes an anxiety attack
That has been lingering
Since the thought of coming here.

Something about the quantity of people
Truly puts my senses on edge
They all funnel through the security lines
Within breathing distance
One by one, by design.
They exemplify our homogenous natures,
Yet our individuality is preserved
Through our relatability with those few
In our traveling company.

Traveling alone is quite a struggle
You must leave all that you love behind
And venture to locations unknown
that you do not wish to go.
Places that you must go,
To provide for those that you love
And hold dear.

Truth be told it's the waiting;
Waiting for your life to move along
So you can board your flight
And continue this journey
We call life.
Waiting is daunting
It foreshadows the realization
That we will all terminate
One day.

...I never really did like airports.

Broken Glass

The mirror stands,
As elegant and beautiful as ever.
Stunning craftsmanship;
The Mahogany frame, engraved
With a soothing floral pattern.

The mirror is true,
Showing at face value.
Reflecting light cast upon its surface,
Faultless

The mirror is scorned,
Enraged by its captivation,
Stones are cast in every direction.
Shattered; ten thousand pieces of
Broken Glass cascade onto the floor.

A man is left with the shards,
Contemplating how to rebuild.
He slowly proceeds to link together,
Piece by piece, hour by hour.

The fragments are bound with his tears,
The frame is shaped from nearby Sequoias,
The engraving is restored with a floral pattern
Which far surpasses the original,
In both beauty and elegance.

The mirror is Reborn.

Drunk on Apathy

It feels as though my mind
Has caged itself into its own prison.
A phantom barrier prevents me
From achieving myself.

Temptress, why do you mock me?
I vehemently desire your light,
But it is a fleeting flicker;
A momentary spark of energy.

The thread she hath woven encompasses my being
Consuming my entirety.
The most intricate maze
Attempts of navigation are futile.

Why have you forsaken me?
Temptress; I fall at your feet
My knees forced into submission
I cannot yield to your wondrous beauty.

Prisoner to my mind,
I cannot escape Her grasp.
She is interwoven with my fate
Unable to separate from the Parasite.

Perhaps one day it will come to fruition
A symbiotic relationship
Welcomed with open arms,
I dream of our Kinship.

Unforgivable Time

My being is consumed with profound emotion
I am at a crossroads from which I do not wish to proceed
One path leads through a forest of sharp needles
The latter; an ominous path through thick brush

O Time, a fickle and unforgiving force
If only I were thine Master
Able to traverse the universe unknown
A boundless life unleashed

The ability to revert
To a time before
No bounty is payment enough
For such power, every being longs for

Why do we live?
What is our purpose?
Fundamentally perplexing
My mortal mind ponders at will

I must accept the inevitable
I cannot confound Time
She is omnipotent and omniscient
She lives outside of mortal bounds

Such is the burden that We support
To carry the weight of our lives
We cannot escape our decisions
We can only embrace them with fervor

Dead Bedroom

Showering alone with my thoughts
Once more.
Water cascades over my skin,
The warmth is familiar and comforting

My eyes blurred
Saturated by the flow
I try to think back,
A time you still desired me.

I cannot discern where the droplets end,
And my tears begin
Just as I cannot determine
When our estrangement first occurred

The pitter-patter of the water
Gives me much needed solace
My mind drifts swiftly,
Succumbing to the notion

The fire that once blazed brightly has been extinguished,
Fizzling into ashes and embers
As we go through the motions
No longer yearning for my affections

Solemn sadness encompasses my being,
Reminiscence of pleasurable moments that once were
The nostalgia of our besotted days,
Drives me deeper into a melancholy stupor.

Endurance

My love for you endures
Like the white Cliffs of Dover
Battered and beaten
By strong, crashing tides

Your beauty is unparalleled
Catching a glimpse
Of your bare, naked body
Is fantasy enough for me

The touch of your skin
Titillates and excites
Caressing your curves
Indulged in pure ecstasy

Our playful banter
We share, back and forth
Brings me sheer joy
I will always treasure

Resilient and determined
As a scholar and professional
Pride wells up inside me
I admire your resolve

Your wonderful face
That gorgeous smile
Lights up the darkest days
Rescuing me from oblivion

My love for you endures
Like time and space
Always growing
Infinite

Conflicted

Where has the time gone
Reminiscing on our exciting moments
Reminded of past thrills and better days,
How I long to return

Return to the past
Relive our blossoming bond
What a simple idea
Yet such an impossible feat

The weeks have past
The void you left inside of me
Grows larger by the day,
Only satiated with mendacious distractions

Enchanting night
Beautiful woman
Thoughts torn asunder
Allegiance in question

Darling of my dreams
Enchantress of the evening
Oh how tempting!
The Road Not Taken

Comfort to the left
Adventure, right
Memories made cherished
Conflicted anticipation of memories to come

Printed in the United States
by Baker & Taylor Publisher Services